PRINCEWILL LAGANG

Building a Lasting Connection

First published by PRINCEWILL LAGANG 2023

Copyright © 2023 by Princewill Lagang

All rights reserved. No part of this publication may be reproduced, stored or transmitted in any form or by any means, electronic, mechanical, photocopying, recording, scanning, or otherwise without written permission from the publisher. It is illegal to copy this book, post it to a website, or distribute it by any other means without permission.

Princewill Lagang asserts the moral right to be identified as the author of this work.

First edition

This book was professionally typeset on Reedsy.
Find out more at reedsy.com

Contents

1	Introduction to Lasting Connections	1
2	Understanding Relationship Foundations	4
3	Effective Communication for Lasting Bonds	7
4	Emotional Intimacy and Vulnerability	10
5	Navigating Challenges and Conflict	13
6	Shared Goals and Values	16
7	Trust and Transparency	19
8	Cultivating Friendship and Fun	22
9	Intimacy and Physical Connection	25
10	Navigating Life Changes Together	28
11	Building a Supportive Partnership	31
12	The Journey of Lasting Connection	34

1

Introduction to Lasting Connections

In a world that's constantly evolving, where technology often takes center stage in our lives, the significance of establishing strong and enduring bonds with others cannot be overstated. This chapter delves into the importance of building lasting connections and explores the myriad benefits they bring to our relationships and overall well-being.

The Significance of Establishing a Strong and Enduring Bond

1.1 The Human Need for Connection

Humans are inherently social beings. From the moment we are born, we seek connections with others. This need for connection is deeply ingrained in our biology and psychology. It's not merely a desire; it's a fundamental requirement for our emotional and psychological well-being.

1.2 Emotional Resilience

Strong and enduring bonds provide a safety net in the stormy sea of life. They offer emotional support during difficult times, helping individuals navigate challenges with greater resilience. Whether it's the comfort of a close friend during a personal crisis or the unwavering support of a family member, these connections play a crucial role in helping us weather life's storms.

1.3 Mental Health Benefits

Studies have consistently shown that people with robust social connections are generally happier and less prone to mental health issues like depression and anxiety. Meaningful relationships provide a sense of belonging and purpose, which can significantly contribute to one's overall mental well-being.

1.4 Personal Growth and Development

Lasting connections also serve as catalysts for personal growth and development. Interacting with diverse individuals exposes us to different perspectives, ideas, and experiences, which can broaden our horizons and encourage self-improvement. A supportive network can motivate us to pursue our goals and aspirations.

Exploring the Benefits of Building Lasting Connections in Relationships

1.5 Enhanced Communication

Establishing and maintaining lasting connections require effective communication skills. When we invest time and effort into nurturing relationships, we naturally become better at listening, expressing our thoughts and feelings, and resolving conflicts constructively. These skills are not only valuable in personal relationships but also in professional settings.

1.6 Trust and Reliability

Lasting connections are built on trust and reliability. When others know they can depend on us, it strengthens the bond. Trust is the foundation of healthy relationships, and it takes time and consistency to establish. However, the benefits, such as a sense of security and mutual support, are well worth the effort.

1.7 Longevity and Depth of Relationships

Lasting connections often lead to deeper, more meaningful relationships. These are the connections that endure through the ups and downs of life, providing a sense of continuity and stability. Such relationships can last for decades, enriching our lives in countless ways.

1.8 Fulfillment and Happiness

Ultimately, the benefits of building lasting connections culminate in a sense of fulfillment and happiness. Meaningful relationships provide joy, laughter, and a profound sense of purpose. They offer a source of emotional sustenance that enriches our lives and makes us feel truly alive.

In the chapters that follow, we will delve deeper into the strategies for nurturing lasting connections, how to overcome common challenges, and the different types of relationships that can benefit from this approach. By the end of this journey, you will have a comprehensive understanding of the profound impact that lasting connections can have on your life and the lives of those around you.

2

Understanding Relationship Foundations

In this chapter, we will delve into the fundamental elements that form the bedrock of strong and lasting connections. Understanding these foundational aspects is essential for nurturing and maintaining healthy relationships. We will explore the core values, trust, and communication skills that underpin lasting connections.

Exploring the Foundational Elements of a Strong Relationship

2.1 Shared Values and Beliefs

One of the key pillars of a strong relationship is a shared set of values and beliefs. These can encompass a wide range of aspects, including moral principles, life goals, and even common interests. When individuals in a relationship align on their fundamental values, it creates a sense of unity and purpose, which strengthens the connection.

2.2 Trust and Reliability

Trust is the cornerstone of any lasting connection. It's built over time through consistent, reliable behavior. Trust means knowing that you can depend on your partner or friend and that they have your best interests at heart. Without trust, relationships are fragile and prone to conflict.

2.3 Effective Communication

Open and effective communication is essential for understanding each other's needs, desires, and concerns. It involves both speaking and listening attentively. Clear communication helps resolve conflicts, prevent misunderstandings, and fosters emotional intimacy.

Identifying the Values, Trust, and Communication at the Core of Lasting Connections

2.4 Core Values in Relationships

Identifying and understanding your own core values is the first step in building lasting connections. Likewise, being aware of your partner's or friend's values is crucial. These values could include honesty, respect, loyalty, empathy, or a shared commitment to personal growth. When values align, it fosters a sense of harmony and connection.

2.5 The Role of Trust

Trust takes time to develop but can be easily eroded. It's vital to be honest, consistent, and dependable in your actions. Trust involves vulnerability, as you allow yourself to rely on another person emotionally. Trust is not just about keeping promises; it's about showing that you can be counted on in both big and small ways.

2.6 Communication as a Bridge

Effective communication bridges the gap between individuals in a relationship. This includes both verbal and non-verbal communication. Listening actively, being empathetic, and expressing your thoughts and feelings honestly contribute to better understanding and connection. Additionally, learning to communicate in times of conflict is crucial for maintaining a healthy relationship.

2.7 Building Emotional Intimacy

Emotional intimacy is a result of values, trust, and communication. It's the deep connection that comes from sharing your innermost thoughts, fears, and dreams with someone you trust. Emotional intimacy is the glue that holds relationships together during difficult times and adds depth and richness during good times.

In the upcoming chapters, we will explore practical strategies for enhancing these foundational elements in your relationships. Whether you're seeking to strengthen an existing bond or form new connections, understanding and applying these principles will help you build lasting and fulfilling relationships.

3

Effective Communication for Lasting Bonds

Effective communication is the linchpin of any strong and lasting connection. In this chapter, we will explore the vital role that communication plays in nurturing relationships. We will also delve into techniques for clear, empathetic, and open dialogue that can strengthen your connections with others.

The Role of Communication in Nurturing a Lasting Connection

3.1 Communication as the Lifeblood of Relationships

Communication is the primary means by which individuals in a relationship understand each other's thoughts, feelings, and needs. It's the lifeblood of a relationship, connecting people on both intellectual and emotional levels. Without effective communication, misunderstandings, conflicts, and emotional distance can take hold.

3.2 Building Trust and Understanding

Effective communication builds trust and understanding. When you express yourself honestly and listen attentively to others, it demonstrates that you value their perspective and are committed to the relationship's success. This, in turn, fosters trust and a sense of being heard and valued.

3.3 Conflict Resolution and Problem-Solving

Conflict is a natural part of any relationship. However, effective communication is the key to resolving conflicts and finding solutions that satisfy both parties. It enables individuals to express their concerns, work through differences, and find common ground, rather than allowing conflicts to escalate and damage the connection.

Techniques for Clear, Empathetic, and Open Dialogue

3.4 Active Listening

Active listening is a foundational skill for effective communication. It involves fully focusing on the speaker, asking clarifying questions, and paraphrasing to ensure you understand their perspective correctly. By demonstrating that you are genuinely engaged, you encourage the speaker to express themselves more openly.

3.5 Empathetic Communication

Empathy is the ability to understand and share the feelings of another person. It's a powerful tool for building emotional connection. To communicate empathetically, acknowledge the other person's emotions, validate their feelings, and show that you care about their well-being. This creates a sense of safety and emotional intimacy.

3.6 Assertive Communication

Being assertive means expressing your thoughts, needs, and boundaries in a clear and respectful manner. It's a balanced approach that avoids passivity (not expressing your needs) or aggression (expressing your needs at the expense of others). Assertive communication promotes honesty and mutual respect in a relationship.

3.7 Non-Verbal Communication

Non-verbal cues, such as body language, tone of voice, and facial expressions, play a significant role in communication. Pay attention to these cues, both in yourself and in others. They can often convey emotions and intentions more powerfully than words.

3.8 Effective Expression

Expressing yourself clearly and concisely is essential. Use "I" statements to express your thoughts and feelings, taking responsibility for your emotions. Avoid blaming or making sweeping generalizations. Be specific and use examples when necessary to illustrate your points.

3.9 Active Conflict Resolution

Conflict is an inevitable part of any relationship. When conflicts arise, approach them with a problem-solving mindset. Focus on the issue at hand, not personal attacks. Collaborate with the other person to find mutually beneficial solutions.

In the chapters ahead, we will delve deeper into specific communication strategies and explore how they can be applied in different types of relationships, from romantic partnerships to friendships and professional connections. By mastering the art of effective communication, you will be better equipped to build and maintain lasting bonds with others.

4

Emotional Intimacy and Vulnerability

In this chapter, we will explore the critical role of emotional intimacy in building and maintaining lasting bonds. We will also discuss the significance of encouraging vulnerability and authentic self-expression within relationships.

The Importance of Emotional Intimacy in Building a Lasting Bond

4.1 Defining Emotional Intimacy

Emotional intimacy refers to the deep connection that arises when individuals in a relationship share their innermost thoughts, feelings, fears, and desires with one another. It's a level of closeness that transcends the superficial and allows for genuine understanding and empathy.

4.2 Enhancing Connection and Trust

Emotional intimacy is a powerful force that enhances the connection and trust between individuals. When you open up and allow someone to see your true self, it creates a profound sense of closeness. This closeness fosters a strong foundation for a lasting bond.

4.3 Navigating Challenges Together

Emotional intimacy becomes particularly vital during challenging times. It provides the emotional support necessary to weather storms and navigate obstacles as a team. Sharing vulnerabilities and seeking comfort in each other's presence can be incredibly comforting and reassuring.

Encouraging Vulnerability and Authentic Self-Expression in Relationships

4.4 Breaking Down Emotional Barriers

Encouraging vulnerability means creating a safe and non-judgmental space where individuals can lower their emotional barriers. This involves being open and honest about your own vulnerabilities and demonstrating empathy and understanding when others do the same.

4.5 Fostering Trust

Trust is closely linked to vulnerability. When you open up and share your authentic self with someone, it demonstrates trust in their ability to handle your emotions with care and respect. Trust is a two-way street, and encouraging vulnerability is a significant step toward building and maintaining trust in a relationship.

4.6 Active Listening and Validation

Active listening, as discussed in Chapter 3, is crucial when encouraging vulnerability. When someone shares their feelings and experiences, listen without judgment, and validate their emotions. Let them know that their feelings are real and important, even if you may not fully understand or agree with them.

4.7 Leading by Example

To encourage vulnerability in others, lead by example. Be willing to share your own vulnerabilities and feelings. This not only sets the tone for open communication but also normalizes vulnerability within the relationship.

4.8 Respect for Boundaries

While encouraging vulnerability is essential, it's equally crucial to respect boundaries. Some individuals may take longer to open up, and that's perfectly okay. Never push someone to share more than they are comfortable with; instead, create an environment where they feel safe to do so at their own pace.

In the subsequent chapters, we will explore specific strategies for deepening emotional intimacy in various types of relationships. By understanding the significance of emotional intimacy and fostering vulnerability and authentic self-expression, you can build and nurture lasting bonds that are both meaningful and fulfilling.

5

Navigating Challenges and Conflict

In this chapter, we will explore the inevitability of challenges and conflicts in any relationship and discuss strategies for handling these situations constructively. By addressing conflicts effectively, you can strengthen the connection in your relationships.

Understanding That Challenges Are a Natural Part of Any Relationship

5.1 The Inevitability of Challenges

Challenges and conflicts are an integral part of any relationship, whether it's a romantic partnership, a friendship, or a professional connection. No two individuals are entirely alike, and differences in personality, values, and goals can lead to disagreements and misunderstandings.

5.2 Normalizing Challenges

It's essential to recognize that encountering challenges does not signify a failing relationship. Instead, it's a normal and healthy part of human interaction. These challenges provide opportunities for growth, understanding, and ultimately, stronger connections.

5.3 The Role of Communication

Effective communication, as discussed in Chapter 3, plays a crucial role in addressing challenges and conflicts. It enables individuals to express their concerns, listen to one another, and work toward solutions. However, it's also essential to approach conflicts with a constructive mindset.

Strategies for Handling Conflicts Constructively and Strengthening the Connection

5.4 Active Listening During Conflict

When conflict arises, active listening becomes even more critical. Ensure that both parties feel heard and understood. Avoid interrupting, and instead, allow each person to express their viewpoint fully. Use empathy to acknowledge their emotions, even if you don't agree with their perspective.

5.5 Maintaining Respect and Empathy

During conflicts, it's easy to become emotionally charged and lose sight of respect and empathy. However, maintaining these qualities is essential. Avoid personal attacks, name-calling, or belittling the other person. Instead, focus on the issue at hand and express your concerns respectfully.

5.6 Seeking Common Ground

Conflict resolution involves finding common ground and mutually acceptable solutions. Explore compromises that take into account the needs and desires of both parties. Be willing to make concessions and prioritize the health of the relationship over being "right."

5.7 Taking a Break When Necessary

In heated conflicts, taking a break can be beneficial. It allows both individuals to cool off, reflect on the situation, and regain emotional composure. Agree on a time to revisit the discussion when you're both in a calmer state of mind.

5.8 Learning From Conflict

Rather than viewing conflicts as negative experiences, consider them opportunities for growth and learning. After resolving a conflict, take time to reflect on what you've both learned about each other and the relationship. This self-awareness can lead to improved communication and understanding in the future.

5.9 Professional Help When Needed

In some cases, conflicts may be deeply rooted or recurring, and professional help, such as couples counseling or mediation, can be valuable. Don't hesitate to seek assistance when you feel that conflicts are straining the relationship beyond your abilities to manage.

By understanding that challenges and conflicts are natural and implementing constructive conflict resolution strategies, you can not only navigate these difficulties but also strengthen the connection in your relationships. In the following chapters, we will delve deeper into specific techniques for enhancing relationships in different contexts and situations.

6

Shared Goals and Values

In this chapter, we will explore the profound impact that shared goals and values can have on cementing a lasting connection. We will also discuss strategies for aligning aspirations and creating a shared vision for the future, which can strengthen your relationships.

The Power of Shared Goals and Values in Cementing a Lasting Connection

6.1 Defining Shared Goals and Values

Shared goals and values refer to the alignment of aspirations and core principles between individuals in a relationship. When two or more people share common objectives and beliefs, it creates a sense of unity and purpose that can deepen the connection.

6.2 Enhancing Connection and Unity

Shared goals and values can enhance the connection between individuals by fostering a sense of unity and partnership. It signifies that you are on the same path, working together towards common objectives. This shared purpose can be a powerful motivator and source of fulfillment in a relationship.

6.3 Providing a Strong Foundation

A shared set of values and goals provides a strong foundation for a lasting bond. It serves as a common reference point during challenging times and a source of inspiration for personal growth and development. This foundation helps individuals weather the storms of life with greater resilience.

Aligning Aspirations and Creating a Shared Vision for the Future

6.4 Identifying Core Values

To establish a shared foundation, it's crucial to identify and discuss your core values with your partner or the people in your relationship. Core values may include honesty, loyalty, family, personal growth, or social justice, among others. Understanding each other's values is the first step toward alignment.

6.5 Setting Common Goals

Once you have a clear understanding of your shared values, you can work on setting common goals. These goals can span various aspects of life, including career, family, personal development, and community involvement. Setting clear, achievable objectives helps give your relationship direction and purpose.

6.6 Creating a Shared Vision

A shared vision is a collective image of the future you want to build together. It involves discussing long-term aspirations, dreams, and the legacy you want to leave behind as a couple or within your relationship. A shared vision can be a source of motivation and a reminder of your commitment to one another.

6.7 Regular Check-Ins

As time goes on, it's essential to have regular check-ins to ensure that your shared goals and values remain aligned. Life is dynamic, and your priorities may evolve. Open and honest communication about your aspirations and any necessary adjustments to your shared vision is crucial for maintaining a strong connection.

6.8 Balancing Individual and Shared Goals

While shared goals and values are essential, it's also crucial to balance them with individual aspirations and autonomy. Encourage each other's personal growth and support pursuits that may not directly align with your shared goals. Finding this balance ensures that both individuals feel valued and fulfilled within the relationship.

In the chapters ahead, we will explore practical techniques for nurturing shared goals and values in various types of relationships, from romantic partnerships to friendships and professional connections. By aligning your aspirations and creating a shared vision, you can strengthen your bonds and build a lasting, fulfilling connection.

7

Trust and Transparency

In this chapter, we will explore the pivotal role that trust plays in building and maintaining connections. We will also discuss strategies for fostering trust through honesty and openness, which are essential components of lasting relationships.

The Essential Role of Trust in Building and Maintaining Connections

7.1 The Foundation of Trust

Trust is the bedrock upon which all strong and lasting connections are built. It is the belief and confidence that individuals have in each other's reliability, honesty, and integrity. Without trust, relationships are fragile and prone to erosion.

7.2 Enhancing Connection and Security

Trust enhances the connection between individuals by creating a sense of security and emotional safety. When you trust someone, you feel comfortable being vulnerable and open, which deepens the emotional intimacy within the relationship.

7.3 Strengthening Resilience

Trust is a source of resilience in relationships. It enables individuals to weather challenges and conflicts with the confidence that they can rely on each other for support and understanding. A foundation of trust helps relationships withstand adversity.

Strategies for Fostering Trust Through Honesty and Openness

7.4 Radical Honesty

Radical honesty involves a commitment to being completely truthful and transparent in your communications with others. It means being honest even when it's uncomfortable or difficult. This level of honesty fosters trust because it shows that you are genuine and forthright in your intentions.

7.5 Consistency and Reliability

Consistency and reliability are essential components of trust. Keep your commitments and promises, both big and small. Be consistent in your actions and behavior over time, so others can rely on you. Consistency builds a sense of predictability and safety in a relationship.

7.6 Open Communication

Open communication is crucial for fostering trust. Encourage an environment where individuals feel comfortable expressing their thoughts, feelings, and concerns without fear of judgment or reprisal. Listen actively and empathetically when others share with you.

7.7 Apologize and Make Amends

Mistakes happen in all relationships. When you make a mistake, take responsibility for it, apologize sincerely, and make amends if necessary. Owning up to your errors and working to rectify them demonstrates your commitment to the relationship's well-being.

7.8 Respect Boundaries

Respecting personal boundaries is a sign of respect and trust. Understand and honor the boundaries set by the people in your relationship. This demonstrates that you respect their autonomy and their right to establish limits.

7.9 Building Trust Over Time

Trust is not built overnight; it evolves over time through consistent, honest, and transparent interactions. Be patient and understanding, recognizing that trust is an ongoing process that requires nurturing and maintenance.

In the chapters ahead, we will delve deeper into practical techniques for building and maintaining trust in various types of relationships. By prioritizing honesty and openness, you can create a strong foundation of trust that fosters lasting and meaningful connections with others.

8

Cultivating Friendship and Fun

In this chapter, we will explore the significance of friendship within lasting connections and discuss how to infuse playfulness, shared experiences, and laughter into your relationships.

Recognizing the Importance of Friendship in a Lasting Connection

8.1 The Friendship Component

Friendship forms the bedrock of many strong and lasting connections, be they romantic, familial, or platonic. A connection that lacks a friendship element can feel shallow, lacking the depth and understanding that true friends share.

8.2 The Unconditional Support of Friendship

Friends provide an unconditional support system. They are there to celebrate your successes, offer a shoulder to lean on during tough times, and provide a non-judgmental space to be yourself. When you cultivate friendship within your relationships, you create a source of unwavering emotional support.

8.3 The Longevity of Friendship

Friendships often endure for years or even a lifetime. They are resilient to the ups and downs of life, offering continuity and stability. Recognizing and valuing the friendship within your connections can contribute to their lasting nature.

Infusing Playfulness, Shared Experiences, and Laughter

8.4 Embracing Playfulness

Playfulness injects joy and lightheartedness into a relationship. It involves engaging in activities purely for fun and enjoyment, without the pressure of achieving specific goals. Playfulness can include anything from spontaneous adventures to playful banter and inside jokes.

8.5 Creating Shared Experiences

Shared experiences create lasting memories and deepen the bond between individuals. Whether it's traveling together, pursuing a hobby, or simply spending quality time, these shared moments strengthen the connection. They provide a sense of togetherness and unity.

8.6 The Healing Power of Laughter

Laughter is a powerful tool for maintaining a healthy and vibrant connection. It reduces stress, enhances mood, and fosters a sense of connection between individuals. Sharing a good laugh can help diffuse tension and strengthen the emotional bond.

8.7 Balance Between Fun and Seriousness

While fun and playfulness are essential, it's also crucial to strike a balance with more serious aspects of a relationship. Recognize when to be there for each other during challenging times and when to support personal growth and development.

8.8 Celebrating Milestones and Traditions

Creating traditions and celebrating milestones together reinforces the connection. Whether it's marking anniversaries, birthdays, or simply acknowledging achievements, these rituals provide an opportunity for reflection and appreciation within the relationship.

8.9 Spontaneity and Surprise

Surprising each other with thoughtful gestures or spontaneous acts of kindness keeps the relationship fresh and exciting. It demonstrates that you value the other person and are willing to put in effort to bring joy to their life.

In the following chapters, we will delve deeper into specific strategies for cultivating friendship and infusing fun into various types of relationships. By recognizing the importance of friendship and incorporating playfulness, shared experiences, and laughter, you can foster lasting and enjoyable connections with others.

9

Intimacy and Physical Connection

In this chapter, we will delve into the multifaceted nature of physical intimacy within lasting connections. We'll explore the different dimensions of physical closeness and discuss strategies for maintaining and enhancing intimacy in your relationships over time.

Exploring the Various Dimensions of Physical Intimacy

9.1 Physical Affection

Physical affection encompasses a wide range of expressions, from holding hands and hugging to cuddling and kissing. These gestures convey love, warmth, and a sense of closeness. Regular physical affection helps maintain a strong emotional bond.

9.2 Sexual Intimacy

Sexual intimacy involves a deep emotional connection expressed through sexual activity. It goes beyond the physical act itself and is characterized by trust, vulnerability, and mutual satisfaction. A satisfying sexual connection can greatly enhance a lasting relationship.

9.3 Non-Sexual Physical Connection

Physical connection isn't limited to sexual activity. Non-sexual physical touch, such as massage, caressing, or simply lying close together, can be equally intimate. It provides comfort, reassurance, and emotional closeness.

9.4 Shared Physical Activities

Participating in physical activities together, whether it's dancing, hiking, or playing sports, fosters a unique kind of physical connection. It encourages teamwork, shared experiences, and the release of endorphins, which can strengthen the bond.

Strategies for Maintaining and Enhancing Intimacy Over Time

9.5 Open Communication

Effective communication is essential when it comes to physical intimacy. Discuss your desires, boundaries, and expectations openly and honestly with your partner. Ensure that both parties feel comfortable expressing their needs and concerns.

9.6 Prioritize Quality Time

Intimacy requires time and attention. Prioritize quality time with your partner, free from distractions. This allows you to connect on a deeper level and create opportunities for physical closeness.

9.7 Spontaneity and Variety

Maintain excitement and novelty in your physical relationship by introducing spontaneity and variety. Surprise your partner with unexpected gestures of affection or explore new experiences together to keep things fresh and exciting.

9.8 Regular Check-Ins

Periodically check in with your partner about your physical connection. Ask how you both feel about it, what could be improved, and what you enjoy most. Open dialogue ensures that you're both on the same page and continuously evolving together.

9.9 Physical Self-Care

Taking care of your physical health and well-being is vital for sustaining physical intimacy. Ensure you have the energy, stamina, and vitality to engage in physical activities with your partner.

9.10 Emotional Connection

Remember that physical intimacy is closely tied to emotional intimacy. Strengthening your emotional connection through open communication, shared experiences, and mutual support enhances the quality of your physical connection.

In the chapters that follow, we will explore specific techniques for cultivating and nurturing physical intimacy within various types of relationships. By understanding the diverse dimensions of physical intimacy and implementing strategies to maintain and enhance it, you can enrich your connections and create lasting, fulfilling relationships.

10

Navigating Life Changes Together

In this chapter, we will explore the challenges and opportunities presented by major life transitions in a relationship. We will discuss strategies for offering mutual support and adapting together, which are essential for maintaining a lasting connection during times of change.

How to Navigate Major Life Transitions as a Couple

10.1 Understanding Life Transitions

Life transitions can encompass a wide range of events, including moving to a new city, changing careers, becoming parents, experiencing the loss of a loved one, or going through personal growth and transformation. These transitions often bring both excitement and stress, and how a couple navigates them can significantly impact their relationship.

10.2 Recognizing the Impact on the Relationship

Major life transitions can place stress on a relationship. They may disrupt established routines and routines, introduce new challenges, and require adaptation and flexibility. However, they also offer opportunities for growth, resilience, and a deepening of the bond between partners.

10.3 Shared Goals and Strategies

Navigating life transitions effectively requires shared goals and strategies. Partners must communicate openly and honestly about their expectations, concerns, and aspirations. Identifying common objectives and working together as a team is key to weathering the storm of change.

Strategies for Offering Mutual Support and Adapting Together

10.4 Communication During Transitions

Open and honest communication is crucial during major life transitions. Share your thoughts, feelings, and concerns with your partner. Actively listen to their perspective and offer empathy and support. Regular check-ins can help both partners stay on the same page.

10.5 Flexible Roles and Responsibilities

Major life changes often require adjustments to roles and responsibilities within the relationship. Be flexible and willing to adapt as needed. Dividing tasks and responsibilities based on each partner's strengths and availability can ease the transition.

10.6 Seeking External Support

Don't hesitate to seek external support when facing challenging life transitions. Whether it's counseling, therapy, or guidance from mentors or support groups, outside help can provide valuable insights and coping strategies.

10.7 Maintaining Self-Care

While supporting your partner is important, it's equally crucial to prioritize self-care during transitions. Ensure that you maintain a healthy balance between your own needs and the needs of the relationship. Taking care of yourself allows you to offer better support to your partner.

10.8 Embracing Change as a Growth Opportunity

View life transitions as opportunities for personal and relational growth. Embrace change with a growth mindset, recognizing that challenges can lead to new strengths, deeper understanding, and a more resilient bond.

10.9 Celebrating Milestones

Acknowledge and celebrate milestones along the way. Recognize achievements, both big and small, that signify progress during the transition. Celebrating together strengthens the connection and provides motivation to keep moving forward.

10.10 Resilience and Adaptability

Above all, remember that resilience and adaptability are key qualities for navigating major life transitions as a couple. Be prepared for setbacks and obstacles, and approach them as opportunities to learn and grow together.

In the chapters that follow, we will explore specific techniques for navigating different types of life transitions within various relationships. By offering mutual support, maintaining open communication, and embracing change as an opportunity for growth, you can navigate major life transitions together and emerge with a stronger and more resilient connection.

11

Building a Supportive Partnership

In this chapter, we will explore the profound value of being each other's biggest cheerleaders and creating a culture of mutual support, encouragement, and empowerment within your relationship.

The Value of Being Each Other's Biggest Cheerleaders

11.1 Support as a Foundation

A supportive partnership is built on the foundation of unwavering encouragement and belief in each other's capabilities. When you actively cheer each other on, it creates an atmosphere of trust and empowerment that strengthens the connection.

11.2 Boosting Confidence

Being each other's cheerleaders boosts confidence and self-esteem. When you know that your partner believes in your abilities and is there to support your endeavors, it empowers you to take on challenges and pursue your dreams with greater enthusiasm.

11.3 Resilience in Adversity

Supportive partnerships are more resilient in the face of adversity. When life throws curveballs, knowing you have someone in your corner provides emotional sustenance and helps you bounce back from setbacks.

Creating a Culture of Mutual Support, Encouragement, and Empowerment

11.4 Active Listening and Affirmation

Active listening is a powerful tool for creating a culture of support. When your partner shares their aspirations or concerns, listen attentively, and offer affirmations and validation. Let them know you understand their perspective and believe in their abilities.

11.5 Constructive Feedback

Offering constructive feedback is an essential aspect of support. When providing feedback, do so with kindness and empathy, focusing on improvement rather than criticism. Frame your feedback as a way to help your partner grow and achieve their goals.

11.6 Shared Goal Setting

Set shared goals and objectives within your relationship. By working together to define your aspirations and action plans, you create a sense of partnership and shared purpose. Celebrate achievements and milestones along the way.

11.7 Supporting Personal Growth

Supportive partnerships encourage personal growth and self-improvement. Encourage each other to pursue hobbies, interests, and education that align with your individual passions. This not only enriches your lives but also deepens your connection as you share in each other's growth.

11.8 Celebrating Each Other's Wins

Celebrate each other's successes, no matter how small they may seem. Whether it's a promotion at work, a personal achievement, or a milestone in a hobby, take time to acknowledge and celebrate these wins together. It reinforces your commitment to each other's happiness and success.

11.9 Embracing Challenges Together

Supportive partnerships do not shy away from challenges; they embrace them together. When facing difficulties, remind each other that you are a team and that you believe in your collective ability to overcome obstacles.

11.10 Empowering Each Other

Empowerment is at the heart of support. Encourage your partner to step outside their comfort zone, pursue their passions, and explore new opportunities. When you empower each other, you both grow stronger and more resilient as a couple.

In the chapters that follow, we will explore specific techniques for building a supportive partnership in various types of relationships, from romantic partnerships to friendships and professional connections. By valuing each other as cheerleaders and fostering a culture of mutual support, encouragement, and empowerment, you can create a deeply fulfilling and lasting connection.

12

The Journey of Lasting Connection

In this final chapter, we will reflect on the journey of building and sustaining a lasting connection and discuss the importance of embracing continuous growth, evolution, and lifelong learning in relationships.

Reflections on the Journey of Building and Sustaining a Lasting Connection

12.1 A Dynamic and Ever-Changing Journey

The journey of building and sustaining a lasting connection is a dynamic and ever-changing one. It's marked by moments of joy, love, and fulfillment, as well as challenges, conflicts, and moments of doubt. Recognizing that this journey is not static but constantly evolving is essential.

12.2 The Power of Connection

Connection is a powerful force that enriches our lives. It provides us with emotional support, companionship, and a sense of belonging. A strong and lasting connection can be a source of immeasurable happiness and fulfillment.

12.3 The Role of Growth and Adaptation

Growth and adaptation are at the heart of a lasting connection. As individuals, you both evolve over time, and so does your relationship. Embracing change, learning from experiences, and adapting together are key factors in sustaining your bond.

Embracing Continuous Growth, Evolution, and Lifelong Learning in Relationships

12.4 Continuous Learning and Self-Reflection

Lifelong learning applies not only to personal growth but also to the growth of your relationship. Continuously seek to understand yourself and your partner better. Reflect on your experiences, challenges, and triumphs as opportunities for learning and growth.

12.5 Open and Honest Communication

Communication remains a cornerstone of a lasting connection. Commit to ongoing, open, and honest communication with your partner. Share your thoughts, feelings, and desires, and actively listen to their perspective. Communication is a lifelong skill that deepens as you both evolve.

12.6 Adapting to Change Together

Life is full of changes, and navigating them together is a testament to the strength of your connection. Whether it's career changes, family dynamics, or personal growth, adapt as a team. Be flexible and willing to support each other through life's twists and turns.

12.7 Celebrate Milestones and Memories

Throughout your journey together, celebrate milestones and create cherished memories. These experiences provide a sense of history and a reminder of the bond you've built. They contribute to the unique tapestry of your relationship.

12.8 Rekindling the Flame

Relationships may go through periods of stagnation or complacency. However, remember that you can always rekindle the flame. Invest in quality time, recommit to shared goals, and rediscover what makes your connection special.

12.9 Gratitude and Appreciation

Practicing gratitude and appreciation is a powerful way to sustain a lasting connection. Express your love and appreciation for your partner regularly. Small acts of kindness and words of gratitude go a long way in maintaining a positive and loving atmosphere.

12.10 Embracing Change Together

Above all, remember that change is a constant in life and in relationships. Embrace change as an opportunity for growth and a chance to deepen your connection. Be curious about each other's evolving interests and passions, and encourage each other to pursue new horizons.

As you continue your journey of building and sustaining a lasting connection, keep in mind that it is a journey of growth, adaptation, and lifelong learning. By embracing change, nurturing your bond with open communication, and celebrating the milestones along the way, you can create a connection that endures the test of time, bringing fulfillment and happiness to both you and your partner.

Conclusion: Building a Lasting Connection

Throughout this journey, we've delved into the intricacies of building and sustaining a lasting connection. We've explored the significance of strong foundations, effective communication, emotional intimacy, and trust. We've discussed the importance of shared goals, laughter, and support in nurturing connections. We've navigated life changes and embraced growth, all with the aim of creating meaningful and lasting bonds.

Building a lasting connection is an art and a science—a delicate balance of love, trust, effort, and understanding. It's a journey filled with moments of joy and triumph, as well as challenges and self-discovery. As we conclude this exploration, let's reflect on some key takeaways:

1. Foundations Matter: A strong and enduring connection begins with a solid foundation of trust, communication, and shared values. These pillars provide stability during turbulent times.

2. Communication Is Key: Open, honest, and empathetic communication is the lifeblood of any lasting relationship. It's the bridge that connects hearts and minds.

3. Embrace Vulnerability: True intimacy blossoms when you allow yourself to be vulnerable and encourage your partner to do the same. Sharing your innermost thoughts and feelings fosters a deep connection.

4. Support and Fun: Celebrate each other's successes, infuse playfulness and shared experiences, and always be each other's cheerleaders. Fun and support are the glue that binds you.

5. Navigate Together: Life is full of changes, and navigating them together strengthens your connection. Embrace change as an opportunity for growth and adaptation.

6. Continuous Growth: Commit to lifelong learning and growth, both individually and as a couple. Embrace change and evolve together.

7. Gratitude and Appreciation: Never underestimate the power of gratitude and appreciation in maintaining a positive and loving atmosphere within your relationship.

Building a lasting connection is a testament to your commitment, resilience, and capacity for love. It's not always easy, but the rewards are immeasurable—a deep sense of belonging, unwavering support, and a partner to share life's joys and challenges.

As you continue on your journey, remember that it's not about reaching a destination but about cherishing the path you travel together. Every moment, every challenge, and every triumph contributes to the tapestry of your connection. Embrace it, nurture it, and watch it flourish into a lasting bond that brings fulfillment and happiness to your life.

www.ingramcontent.com/pod-product-compliance
Lightning Source LLC
LaVergne TN
LVHW021055100526
838202LV00083B/5973